Everything Real Justin Bieber Fans Should Know & Do

Barry MacDonald

TRIUMPH
BOOKS

This book is available in quantity at special discounts for your group or organization. For further information, contact:

Triumph Books LLC
814 North Franklin Street
Chicago, Illinois 60610
Phone: (312) 337-0747
www.triumphbooks.com

Printed in U.S.A.
ISBN: 978-1-60078-770-6

Content packaged by Mojo Media, Inc.
Joe Funk: Editor
Jason Hinman: Creative Director

Introduction

The biggest name in pop music today, Justin Bieber has conquered all in just a few short years. With a string of records that have topped the charts and sold millions of copies, singles all over the radio, hundreds of different merchandise items and a social media presence that's one of the biggest in the world, Justin is truly a household name.

It's hard to believe that all of Justin's success started with something as simple as a YouTube channel. His natural musical ability was clear to everyone who saw those early videos, so it's no surprise that he's as big as he is today. Justin might not have been groomed for success under the watchful eyes of a Hollywood studio, but his talent overcame any hurdles in his way.

There's no bigger pop star than Justin Bieber. He can even make new pop stars come out of thin air with just a few tweets: his discovery of Carly Rae Jepsen led directly to her reaching No. 1 with "Call Me Maybe." With the release of his new album *Believe*, it's clear that Justin is going to be the world's leading pop star for years to come. He's as genuine as can be; a true talent making the most of his chances, but there might be a few things that fans still need to learn about their favorite singer.

Justin's mom wanted to share his singing talents with family members

Justin's mom, Pattie, started posting videos of Justin singing on YouTube in 2007 and the world stood up and took notice. Before long, "kidrauhl," his YouTube channel, was getting hits from random strangers—lots of them! One of those viewers was Scooter Braun, an Atlanta-based party promoter and fledgling music producer. He saw something special in the baby-faced Canadian singer—a kid who could belt an anthem from Aretha Franklin as well as master the neo-soul of contemporary pop artists like Chris Brown and Lil Bow Wow.

number 2

Justin Bieber is not your typical teenager

In fact, he's not even your typical recording artist. He's never acted on Nickelodeon. He never had a show on the Disney Channel. He doesn't have a blond alter ego—well, at least when he's not pranking his audience. He isn't a boy-bander or a Jonas Brother or even a little bit Raven. What he is, however, is the first bona fide Internet music success story. Armed with a video camera and a computer, he leveraged his best asset—his natural talent—all the way to superstardom.

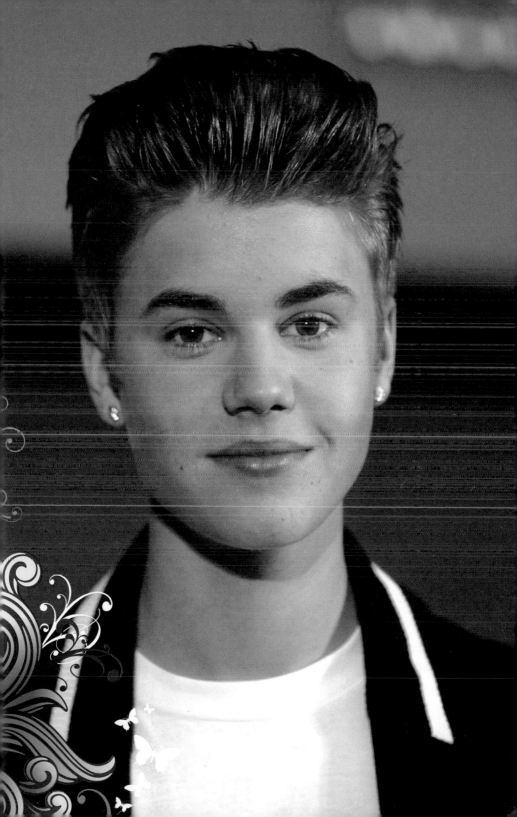

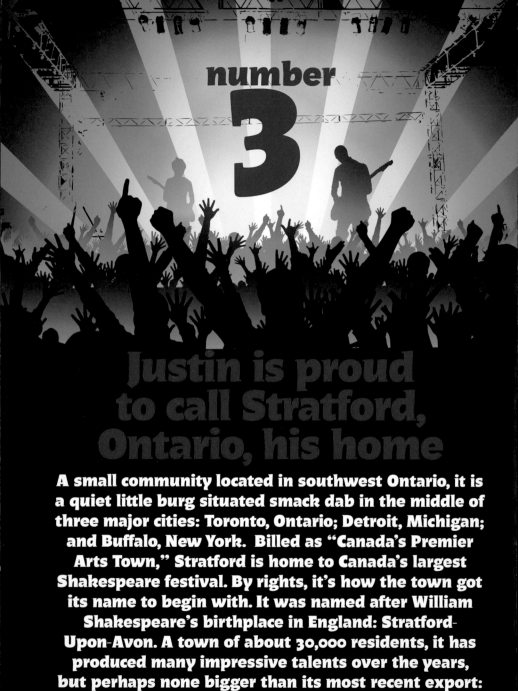

number
3

Justin is proud to call Stratford, Ontario, his home

A small community located in southwest Ontario, it is a quiet little burg situated smack dab in the middle of three major cities: Toronto, Ontario; Detroit, Michigan; and Buffalo, New York. Billed as "Canada's Premier Arts Town," Stratford is home to Canada's largest Shakespeare festival. By rights, it's how the town got its name to begin with. It was named after William Shakespeare's birthplace in England: Stratford-Upon-Avon. A town of about 30,000 residents, it has produced many impressive talents over the years, but perhaps none bigger than its most recent export: Justin Bieber.

"Canada is an awesome country in general, and Stratford is an excellent place to call home," writes Bieber in *First Step 2 Forever*. "The people are nice, but not easily impressed."

number
4

Justin had a happy, active childhood

Justin Drew Bieber was born to parents Pattie Mallette and Jeremy Bieber, and to hear him tell it, he was just a regular Canadian kid. "I love hockey, maple syrup, and Caramilk bars," he wrote in *First Step 2 Forever*. He hung out with his friends, skateboarding, telling jokes, playing soccer and basketball, and—like most every Canadian boy—he thought hockey was king. Justin played center forward on his local team, the Stratford Warriors. Whether it was a stick and a puck, a skateboard, a basketball, or a soccer ball, he just loved being active.

number 5

Justin was captivated by music from an early age

In a revealing scene in *Justin Bieber: Never Say Never*, family videos capture a very auspicious moment in his childhood. It depicts a young Justin sitting by the Christmas tree. His eyes light up as he opens the present: a bongo drum. He begins banging on it enthusiastically, putting on a show for the crowd surrounding him. As a fledgling drummer, he's not half bad. As a fledgling entertainer? You can tell he's got it.

"I always knew Justin was gifted. Even as a one-year-old who was barely standing, I remember him banging on tables, banging in rhythm," his mom told *Vanity Fair*.

number

6

There was always music in Justin's house

If Pattie wasn't playing it on the radio, there were musicians in the house. Many of her friends were musicians and played in the praise band at their local church. In an effort to encourage his apparent musicality, they encouraged Justin to join in with them. Quick to bang on a drum, he played happily along with the music. "Sometimes the percussionist would let me play with the various noisemakers. When he saw that I wanted to play—not just play—he'd let me sit on his knee while he played on the drum kit," Justin writes in his memoir. "After a while, he handed me the sticks and let me have a go at it."

number

7

Justin's first performance in public was in a singing contest in Stratford

The town announced that in January 2007 it would hold a singing competition in the mold of *American Idol*. The competition was put on by the local YMCA, a spot where Justin frequently played basketball. Even among the local participants in the Stratford Star contest, he was different. He had no formal training. He had not participated in a choir or other singing group. He was considerably younger—just 12 years old. As soon as he opened his mouth and that big voice rang out, people knew Justin was for real. He made it all the way to the finals but ultimately missed out on the grand prize.

number 8

Justin's confidence grew as a singer after the competition

By this time also an ace on the guitar, he began taking his act to the streets of Stratford. He could often be found busking in front of the Avon Theatre during the town's summer tourist season. Still covering other artists, his list of songs was growing by the day. On any given day, you might hear anything from country groups like Rascal Flatts to Christian artists like Jennifer Knapp.

Around the same time, Justin's mom had a bright idea about starting a YouTube channel. The rest, as they say, is history.

number
9

On January 19, 2007, "kidrauhl" was born on YouTube

"The next thing we knew, all these strangers were clicking onto it, probably because they recognized the song. Then it was 'Oh, he's so cute,' and then, 'Why don't you sing this song or that song?' I said 'Oh, they want you to sing this song—let's try,'" Pattie told *Vanity Fair*. Pattie uploaded more...and more. "It was a horrible camera; I'm a terrible cameraman; it was awful sound, very raw video—but I put them up. Then it was 'Oh look, honey, you have a hundred views.' Then 'Oh wow, a thousand views.'... Next thing we knew, thousands and thousands of views. But it never once occurred to me that there would be a music career out of this."

number 10

More than just fans were watching Justin on YouTube

Justin started getting the attention of music executives, many of whom contacted Pattie with offers of management and promises of riches. It all sounded too good to be true—and Pattie wasn't buying it.

Then came Scooter Braun. Recalling the first time he saw Justin online, he told the *Hollywood Reporter,* "I heard the tone in his voice and I saw some instrumentation and it was just raw talent. And my gut went crazy.... It was a feeling I had when I was watching. This is it. This is what I had been looking for. And then I became completely obsessed with tracking him down."

number
11

Scooter Braun had a hard time getting a meeting with Justin

After a lot of persistence, he finally convinced Pattie to meet him halfway; she and Justin would fly out to Atlanta to meet with him, but no with strings attached. By the end of the visit, Pattie knew they had found their man.

As it turned out, Scooter and Justin were a match made in heaven. The manager had a brilliant plan to build the singer's platform. He had raised his platform so much with YouTube already, and they worked together to continue building that fan base. He started to take Justin around to meet with local radio DJs and executives.

number 12

There are many temptations with being a celebrity

Life in the fast lane certainly has its pitfalls. And early stardom is especially tricky to adjust to. For many young celebrities, fame can mean easy access to drugs, alcohol, and other dangerous influences. In today's gossip-magazine culture, the examples aren't difficult to find—they're everywhere.

Bieber's mentor Usher, who knows a thing or two about resisting fame's temptations as a young man, has a pragmatic view. "The pitfalls of fame come in time...[but Justin's career] should be a long story, which is what we hope for. We hope for longevity," he told CNN.

number
13

Justin has strong people around him to help him handle his stardom

Keeping it all together for Justin is about his faith, but more important, it's about the people with whom he surrounds himself.

In an interview with the Associated Press, he explained how his faith in God helps him keep perspective. "Hollywood is...a scary place. There's a lot going on, there's a lot of bad things, but there [are] also a lot of good things. I'm able to live my dream. I'm able to do a lot of good things."

number
14

Manager Scooter Braun is also an important presence in his life

A former party promoter, Scooter has the right perspective on the scene and how easily people can fall into it. He shed some light on why this singer might be the exception to the spoiled-young-Hollywood rule in an interview with MTV News. "Justin doesn't study the people who made it; he studies the people who haven't. He hears all the naysayers about how he's going to disappear, so he likes to look up people who used to be the so-called Justin Biebers before him and didn't go anywhere. He wants to see why they didn't go anywhere."

15

Vocal coach "Mama" Jan Smith is Justin's self-described "secret weapon"

"She's one of the greatest people in the world," Justin wrote in his autobiography, *First Step 2 Forever*. "She's like a second mom to all of us, and she's become one of the most important people in my life." Plus, she keeps him honest. "She doesn't mess around," he continues. In spite of all the glitz and glamour, those who surround Justin are determined to provide some sense of normalcy for him.

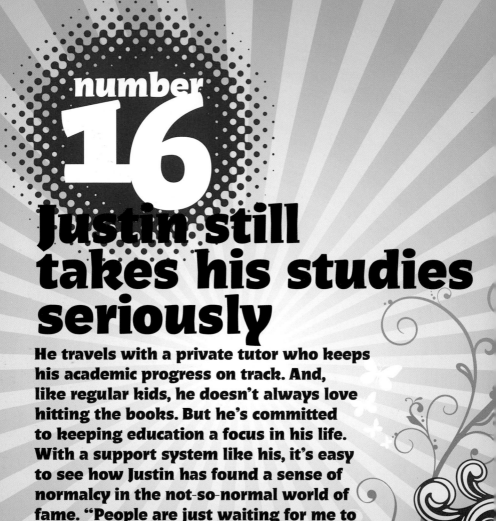

number 16

Justin still takes his studies seriously

He travels with a private tutor who keeps his academic progress on track. And, like regular kids, he doesn't always love hitting the books. But he's committed to keeping education a focus in his life. With a support system like his, it's easy to see how Justin has found a sense of normalcy in the not-so-normal world of fame. "People are just waiting for me to personally mess up. But I'm just a regular person," Justin told *Vanity Fair*.

Deep down, Justin is a normal kid living a very, very abnormal life

In a 2011 interview with Ellen DeGeneres, Justin made his case. "When people say I'm not normal it's wrong because I'm as normal as it gets.... I hang out with my friends. I go to the movies." The singer has said that the hardest thing about his job is being on the road full-time. "I miss hanging out with my friends at school but having this opportunity is so great, it's a once-in-a-lifetime opportunity, it's definitely worth it."

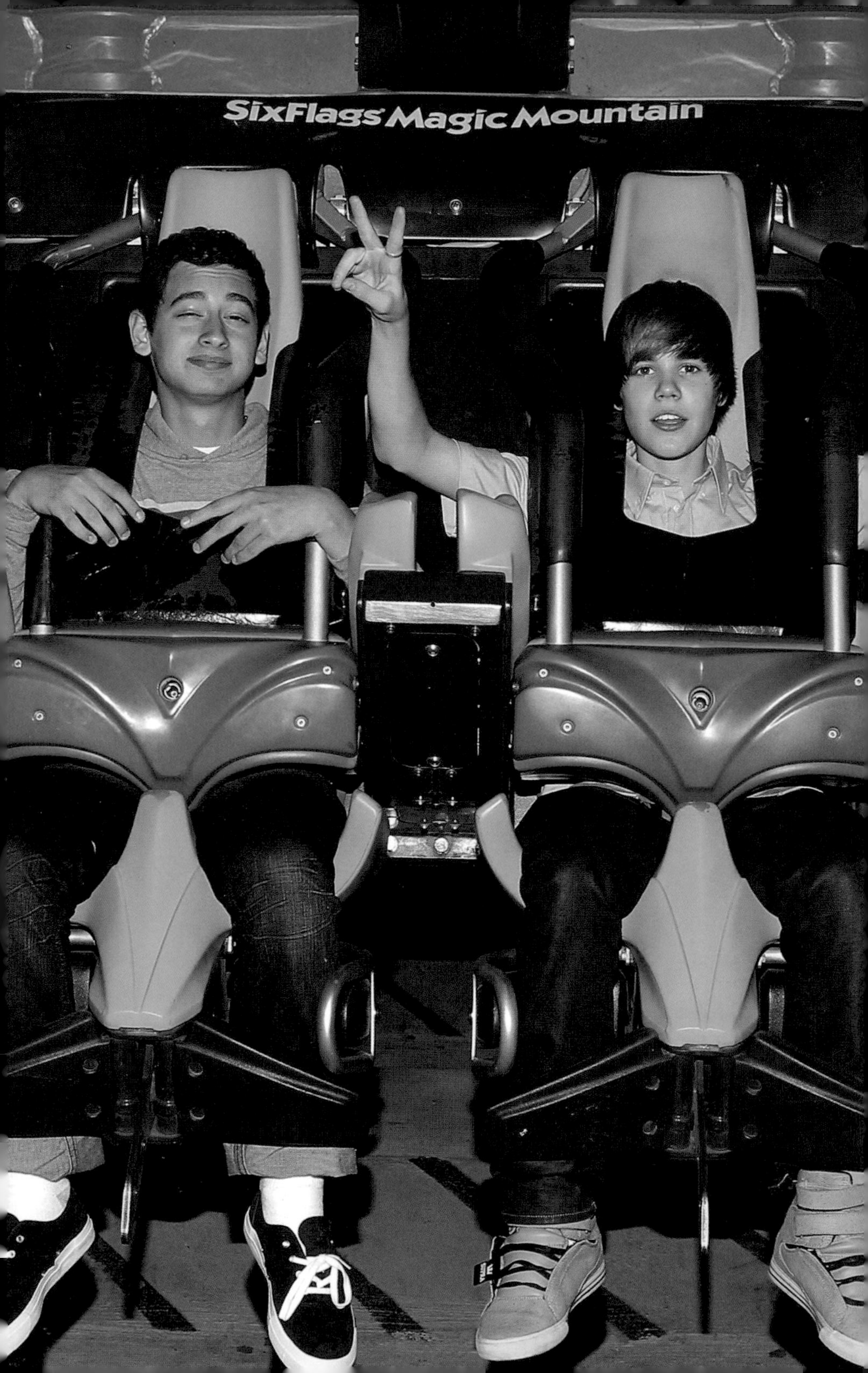
SixFlags Magic Mountain

18

Justin works hard to stay in touch with his friends

With a demanding schedule that sees him away from home more often than not; it's hard for Justin to keep up with his friendships. Thanks to technology like text messages, e-mail and video chats he's able to keep a close eye on what's happening in LA and back home in Stratford.

Justin only sees his best friends from Stratford every now and then, but whenever they do they enjoy doing normal stuff like shooting hoops, skateboarding, playing video games and just hanging out. They enjoy making trips to come visit Justin, which always include something fun like hanging out with other big-name artists like Eminem.

number
19

Justin's days on the road usually start with school

Justin's tutor travels with him wherever he goes. He's committed to his goal to go to college one day. One of the advantages of having a tutor while traveling: he gets to learn the history of the places he visits while he's there.

Predictably, he likes school about as much as most students do. Sometimes he just wants to "throw erasers at the teacher's head." And maybe he likes to play the occasional prank on his tutor, Jenny, too—although he tries to keep the schoolwork balanced with the merrymaking.

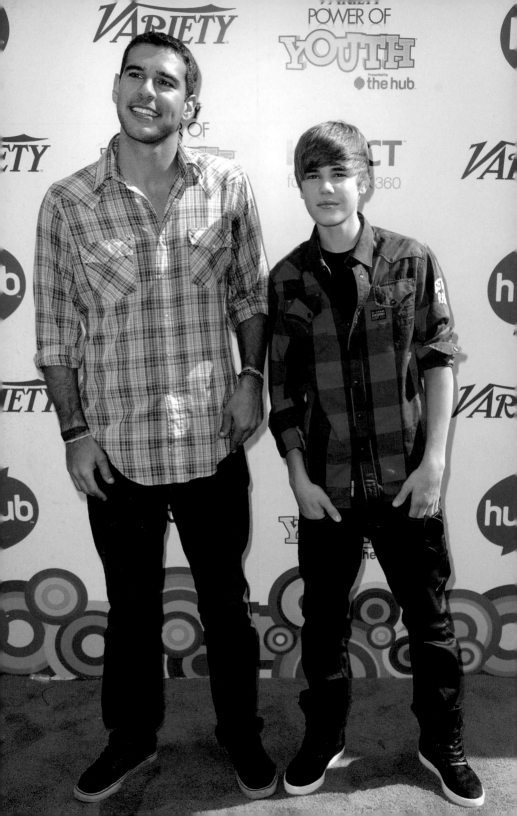

Even though he doesn't always like school, Justin knows the value of education

In fact, one of the causes closest to his heart is Pencils of Promise, an organization that helps to build schools in underdeveloped countries. The charity's mission is to provide education for those among the 75 million children worldwide who do not have access to schooling. Justin is one of the charity's biggest supporters and is closely involved with it.

number

21

Girls are one of Justin's favorite distractions

He knows what he likes in a girl. "I like girls who are outgoing and funny, someone who's smart that I can have a good conversation with," the singer has said. "I don't like girls who wear lots of makeup and you can't see their face. Some girls are beautiful but insecure and look much better without the makeup, but decide to put loads on. I like girls with nice eyes and a nice smile." Sorry though, ladies, Justin has been dating Selena Gomez for years.

number 22

Justin loves taking time to just clown around

Readers of his Twitter page know it all too well. Among the serious messages he posts to his Twitter feed—from updates about music and appearances to inspirational messages to fans—he's also quick with a joke.

In 2010, Justin helmed the popular comedy website, FunnyorDie.com, which was created by funnymen Will Ferrell and Adam McKay. As an April Fool's Day prank, Bieber "took over" the site, saying, "It's mine. I bought it. Now it's BieberorDie. Anything that's not Bieber...dies." In the hilarious clip, he extols the virtues of being Justin Bieber: "I talk loudly in libraries. I swim directly after I eat. I don't care."

number

23

Justin enjoys letting his comedic side show, and he's very funny

Later in 2010, Justin popped up on the long-running late-night comedy show *Saturday Night Live*. Scheduled as the musical guest, Bieber made a few cameos in the show's sketches, including a hilarious bit in which he was the object of his high school teacher's affection. Proving that he could poke fun at himself and his heartthrob image, Bieber winked and tossed his hair at the smitten teacher, played by Tina Fey, throughout the sketch.

His appearance went over so well that he was invited back to *SNL*

He returned in 2011 to join guest host Dana Carvey in two very funny sketches. The first, a revival of Carvey's beloved "Church Chat," saw Justin leading the Church Lady herself into temptation. In the other, a fake movie trailer making fun of films like the then-new-release *The Roommate*, Justin stars as a college student who just might be the object of his creepy roommate's obsession. "This isn't going to be one of those things where our friendship starts out fine but then you get really possessive and crazy because I'm not really up for that," Justin tells Andy Samberg in the clip.

Justin has crossed over into the world of late-night news comedy

In February 2011 he took over the biggest show in the genre, sitting in for Jon Stewart on *The Daily Show*. In a spoof of body-swapping movies like *Freaky Friday* and *Vice Versa*, the two pretend to be trapped in the other's bodies. Bieber, playing Jon Stewart, agrees to switch back bodies, but not before he fondles his own hair one last time. "It's just so natural. It's just so pure," he jokes.

Jimmy Fallon is frequently the target of Bieber's humor

Justin has appeared on his show several times, and each time the two have produced comedy gold. In a recent spoof of Bieber's television commercial for the fragrance Someday, Fallon enters the scene as an "older, fatter" version of the Biebs. "What happened?" Bieber asks. "You just got busy. And your metabolism changed a bit," Fallon responds.

"I can eat like five slices of pizza and I don't gain an ounce," the incredulous singer says. "Well, enjoy it, dude," Fallon admonishes.

Justin would like to star in a movie one day

Recently, the Hollywood casting rumors have been swirling. Some say he is in talks to star in a forthcoming Ashton Kutcher movie. Kutcher's former show *Punk'd* is getting a reboot on MTV this year, and Justin appeared on the new version's season premiere—pranking fellow musician and friend Taylor Swift. But he won't take on permanent hosting duties on the series.

With his natural on-screen charisma and indisputable sense of humor, Bieber could be bound for silver-screen stardom. After all, he's already broken the bank with his concert documentary movie *Justin Bieber: Never Say Never.*

number
28

Justin's music roots are wide-ranging

As comfortable with Sarah McLachlan as with Stevie Wonder, his interests growing up ranged far and wide. You can hear it in his performances. He delivered his Stratford Star performance of "Respect" with a confidence worthy of the Queen of Soul Aretha Franklin herself. His rendition of Edwin McCain's heartbreak anthem "I'll Be" was imbued with a sadness the then-12-year-old couldn't possibly have experienced personally.

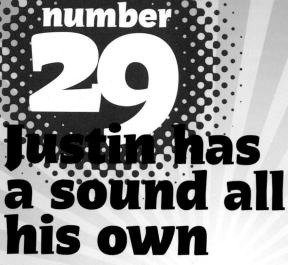

number 29

Justin has a sound all his own

"I've never tried to sound like anybody," he told *McLean's* magazine. He's said that the worst thing he could hear about himself is to be described as a carbon copy of somebody else. Even as a youngster, he possessed the most precious vocal gift a singer could have: the ability to infuse emotion into song. His vast musical education started at home with his mom. Between the pop songs of the day they heard played on the radio and the contemporary Christian music they heard from the praise band at their church on Sundays, there were a lot of different sounds at work.

number
30

Instruments were all around Justin's house

"By the time I was four or five, I could climb up on the stool and play the [drum] kit all by myself, and, about that same time, I discovered I could get up on the piano bench and pound on that, too," he writes in *First Step 2 Forever.* "Much to everyone's surprise, it started sounding like actual music."

Jeremy Bieber picked up on his son's love of music, too, and shared his love of rock 'n' roll with his son. Soon Justin was strumming chords from Bob Dylan's "Knockin' on Heaven's Door" with his dad. A whole new avenue of music opened up. After Dylan came the full-throttle guitars of Jimi Hendrix, Aerosmith, and Van Halen.

number

31

Michael Jackson is Justin's biggest influence

"Michael was able to reach audiences from young to old; he never limited himself. He was so broad, everybody loved him, and that's what my goal is—to basically make people happy, to inspire them, and to have everyone root for me," Justin told *Vanity Fair*.

And certainly, there are parallels between the two artists. Jackson's recording career began at an early age, too. Along with his siblings as the group the Jackson Five, he recorded his first record at age 10. Navigating worldwide fame is no easy feat, but he was able to translate his success as a child star into unparalleled success as an adult performer.

Justin's other influences are wide-ranging and often change

He thinks the Beatles, Jackson, and Tupac are among the best ever. He also cites Prince and Ozzy Osbourne—two very different performers both known for their outsized stage presence—as influences. Bieber also likes fellow chart-toppers Rihanna, Lil Wayne, Drake, Chris Brown, and Sean Kingston. (Brown and Kingston are friends and collaborators.) And Kanye West—who recently worked with Justin to produce a remix of Bieber's "Runaway Love" featuring Raekwon of the Wu-Tang Clan—is also a fave. He's also a big fan—and friend—of multiplatinum singer-songwriter Taylor Swift.

33

Justin owes much of his breakout success to the Internet

When Pattie posted those first YouTube videos of Justin singing at the Stratford Star, Justin became more than just a local singer. People from all over the world were watching. As Justin's videos began to gain popularity, he began to get the attention of people within the music industry. Before Justin, the careers of young musicians followed a predictable pattern. It was difficult for an artist to emerge without a traditional platform. The typical springboard was television, and most of the young stars to emerge in the '90s—singers like Miley Cyrus and the Jonas Brothers—were supported by their shows on children's cable networks such as the Disney Channel or Nickelodeon.

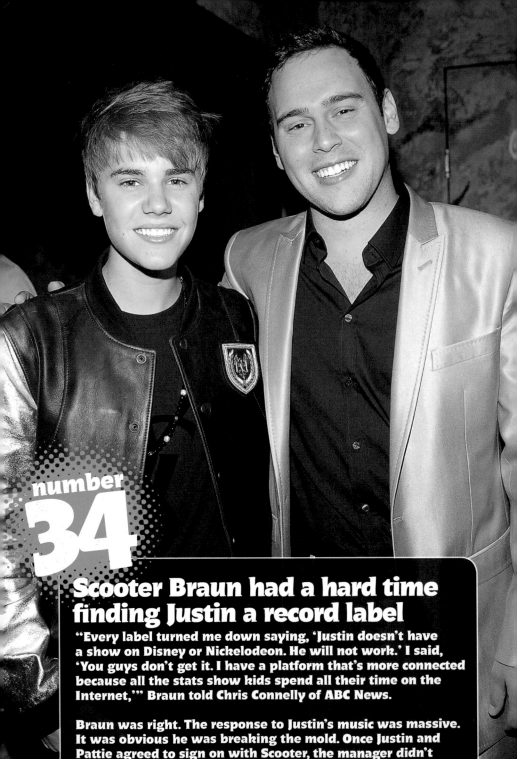

Scooter Braun had a hard time finding Justin a record label

"Every label turned me down saying, 'Justin doesn't have a show on Disney or Nickelodeon. He will not work.' I said, 'You guys don't get it. I have a platform that's more connected because all the stats show kids spend all their time on the Internet,'" Braun told Chris Connelly of ABC News.

Braun was right. The response to Justin's music was massive. It was obvious he was breaking the mold. Once Justin and Pattie agreed to sign on with Scooter, the manager didn't angle for a television vehicle. Instead, he put together a plan to increase Justin's Internet presence even further.

Justin is way more accessible than most pop stars

From the start, he communicated directly with fans on YouTube and, later, Twitter. He read and responded to his fan mail. He was no Hollywood-created confection; he was a real person with real dreams and aspirations.

The efforts helped humanize Justin to a fan base that couldn't ordinarily have interaction with other artists. Looking back, there is little doubt that the unconventional marketing strategy helped the musician to land his record deal.

number

36

Few people are as influential on the Internet as Justin

His albums and singles have consistently charted among iTunes' top downloads. Small wonder, then, that he was named one of *Time* magazine's 100 Most Influential People of the Year. He was also 2010's Most Influential Twitter Celebrity according to *Forbes* magazine, besting rival recording artist Lady Gaga.

He has used the Internet as a way to keep fans around the world on the cutting edge of all things Biebs, announcing everything from appearances to new projects to inspirational messages for his fans. It's his way to make every fan feel like he or she is an insider.

PEREZ HILTON
LifeStyles Condoms
Alizé
PEREZ HILTON
PEREZ HILTON
PEREZ HILTON
PEREZ HILTON

number
37

Justin likes to reveal details of his albums and videos online

In anticipation of the release of *My World 2.0*, Justin kept his followers in the loop by tweeting updates on the album release on a on a near-daily basis. The marketing efforts worked. *My World 2.0* sold more than one million copies in presale—that is, before the CD was even in stores.

Music videos, once strictly the province of music-television networks like MTV, are another huge Internet draw for Bieber. His videos are among the tops on streaming sites like Vevo and download sites such as iTunes.

38

Justin uses the Internet to call attention to his favorite charities

In the aftermath of the Japanese earthquakes, many celebrities took to the Internet to rally support for the many victims of the tragedy. Bieber encouraged his own fans to donate to the Red Cross' relief efforts. He has also raised awareness and generated donations for Pencils of Promise, an organization with which he is directly involved that helps further worldwide education.

number
39

Justin's mastery of Twitter got him a hit single

Kanye West, writing on his own Twitter feed, tweeted, "Listening to Justin Bieber 'Run Away Love' [sic]. I love Sunday mornings in the crib.... This song is the jam." Bieber caught Kanye's tweet and responded with thanks for the shout-out.

"So bugged out that me and @justinbieber are tweeting at the same time... Social networking is pretty awesome," Kanye continued. As it turned out, the chance conversation was indeed an awesome coincidence. Two weeks later, West's remix of "Runaway Love" featuring Raekwon was completed. The single was a success for all three artists.

Justin once used the Internet to help a kid who was being bullied

Australian teenager Casey Heynes went online to lash out at bullies who were physically and verbally tormenting him at school on a daily basis. The video caught the attention of Justin, and the singer reached out to Heynes, flying the teenager and his family to attend the star's concert in Melbourne. The video depicts Heynes fighting back against his attackers.

Bieber, who has long been vocal about stopping teenage bullying, alerted his Twitter followers to Heynes' plight: "This is Casey the punisher...a kid who stood up for himself against bullying. A real life hero."

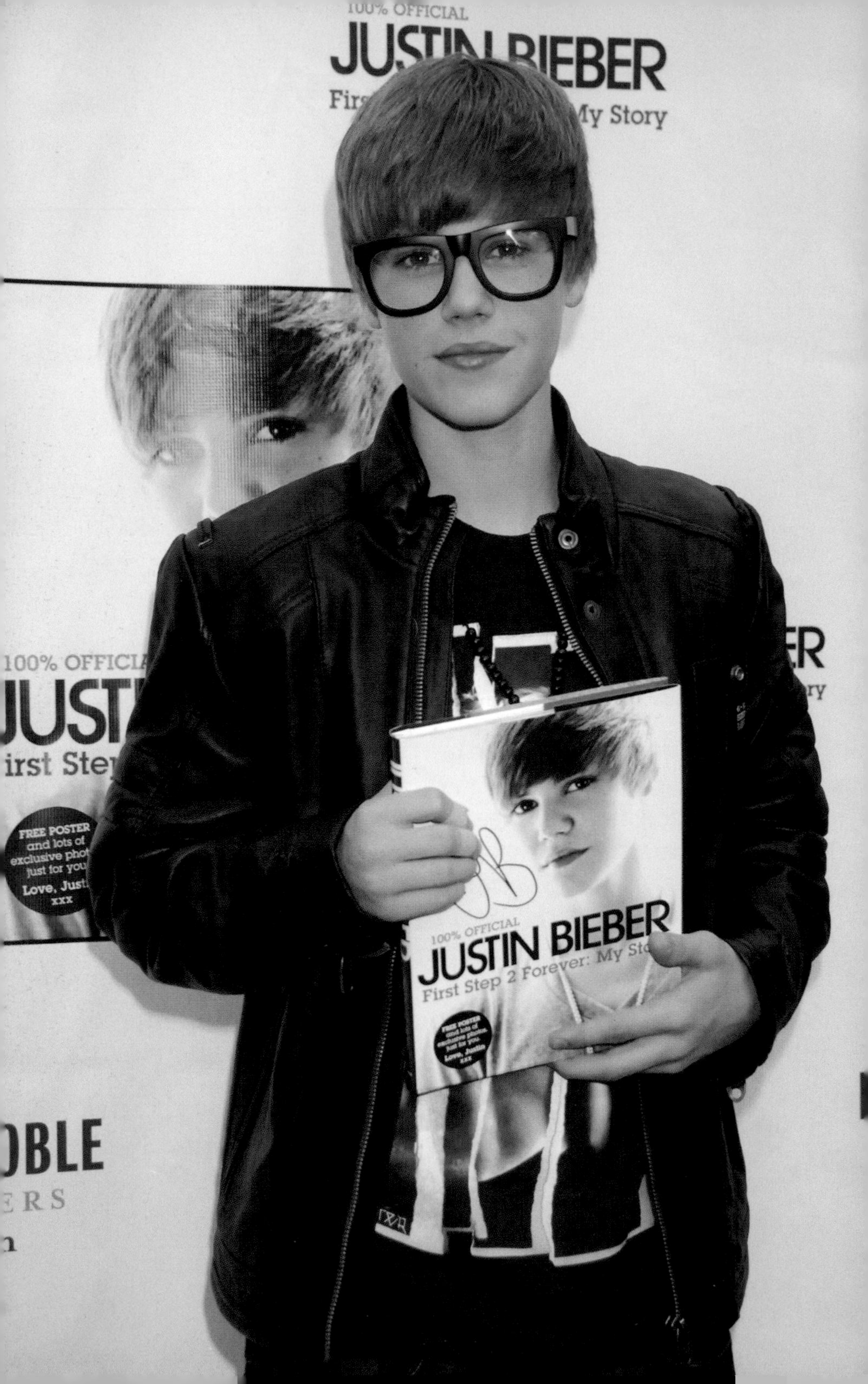
100% OFFICIAL
JUSTIN BIEBER
FREE POSTER
and lots of

number 41

Justin's autobiography was released in 2010

The book tells Justin's life story in his own words, revealing the portrait of a very humble, self-possessed musician on the rise.

It should come as no surprise to Justin's fans that the story begins with them. The singer seems always to put his fans front and center. The book opens with a dedication to his faithful, who he calls "the greatest fans in the world." He writes, "Every one of you is 'My Favorite Girl' for a different reason, because each of you is special in your own way. Everywhere I go, whatever I do, I try to connect with as many of you as possible."

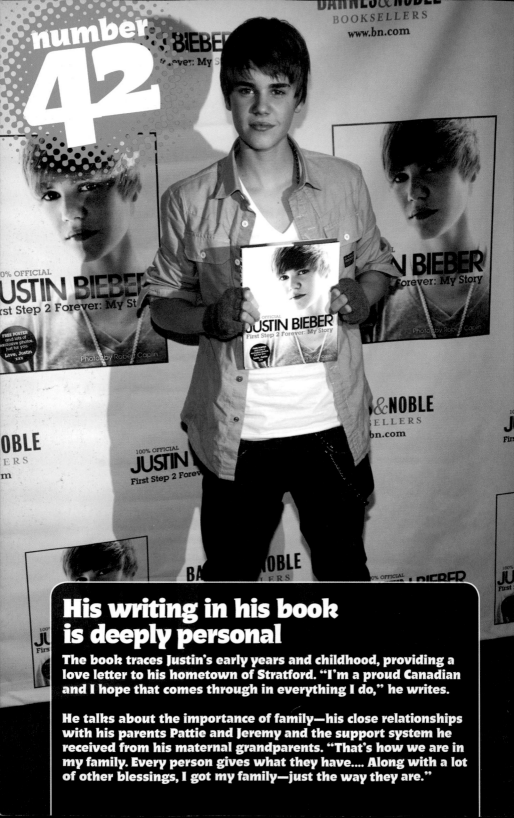

His writing in his book is deeply personal

The book traces Justin's early years and childhood, providing a love letter to his hometown of Stratford. "I'm a proud Canadian and I hope that comes through in everything I do," he writes.

He talks about the importance of family—his close relationships with his parents Pattie and Jeremy and the support system he received from his maternal grandparents. "That's how we are in my family. Every person gives what they have.... Along with a lot of other blessings, I got my family—just the way they are."

Justin has written about his parents' split and how it affected him

Showing a remarkable maturity, he understands the realities that contributed to the split. "My mom and dad were in their late teens when I was born... My dad was basically a kid, doing his best to handle huge responsibilities. Lately, I've started to understand how hard that is."

He praises his mom for allowing him to find his calling in life and encouraging him to play music. To him, that encouragement was the one thing that fostered his emergence as a musician beyond any other influence.

Justin was still unknown around Stratford until Scooter Braun made him locally famous

He had appeared in Stratford Star, but most of the people in his town still didn't know that he sang. Braun, who was desperate to land the young musician as a client, had made a phone call to Justin's school, and the die was cast. Administrators discovered Justin's YouTube offerings and suddenly realized they had a celebrity in their midst. They put together a montage of YouTube clips to play during the morning announcements. "Kids had no idea I did music. They didn't hang out at the tourist places where I was busking."

Braun and Bieber knew they had something special from the start

Reflecting on the connection they had in that first conversation, Justin writes, "Sure, he was young, but he was polite and super-motivated. He knew a lot about the business. And he believed in me."

As history has proven, Scooter's instincts were right. In no time at all, Justin was signed to a record deal, climbing the charts, and embarking on a world tour across five continents. "It was crazy.... Suddenly the whole world was paying attention," he writes.

Usher is one of Justin's biggest mentors

The singer offered him some sage advice as he embarked on his first world tour. "The successful journey starts with the first step. And obviously that first step is the hardest. It's a lot to ask of someone so young to take on such an incredible feat. You've got to pace yourself. Enjoy yourself. Go out there and know that all this hard work has paid off, and this is the moment for you to enjoy it."

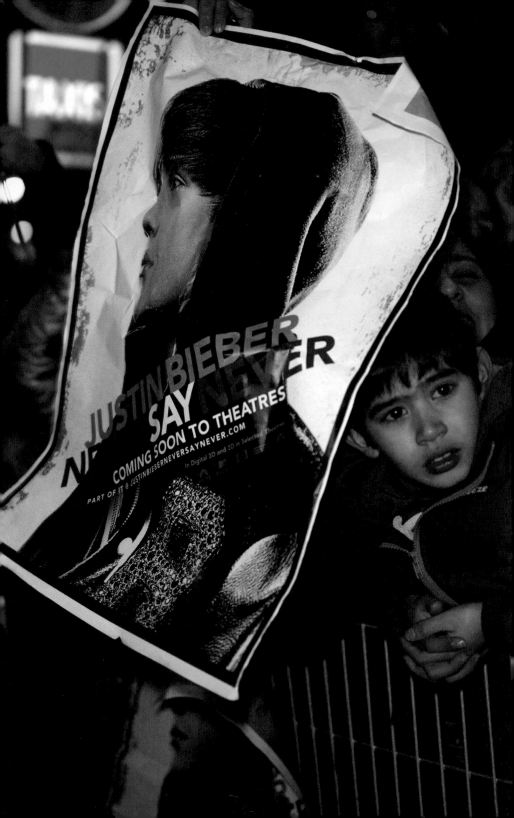

number
47

Much of Justin's writing centers around life on the road

This gives readers a real inside look at what it's like to be on tour for months at a time. Photographs by Robert Caplin provide candid shots of life on tour and are a visual companion to Justin's words.

"Traveling has definitely opened my eyes to different cultures and the way people see things.... [It] has taught me more than any school ever taught me. And I've done more geography than most students," he writes.

number
48

Justin knows he is a 'rags-to-riches' story, and it keeps him humble

"The success I've achieved comes to me from God, through the people who love and support me, and I include my fans in that. Every single one of you lifts me a little higher."

If the aim with his book was to inspire his fans to reach for their own dreams, Justin hit the mark perfectly. The book's closing words are Justin's own mantra and a call to arms for all dreamers: "never say never."

number

49

Justin's movie came out weeks before his 17th birthday

Opening in the usually quiet month of February, the movie was a runaway success. According to the authoritative website BoxOfficeMojo.com, the film is the third-highest-grossing documentary film ever released.

Far from being a typical concert documentary like some of its recent predecessors—including Miley Cyrus and the Jonas Brothers' 3-D offerings—Justin's film sets out to tell the full story of the artist and his musical education.

number 50

Justin's grandfather reflects on his early talent in the movie

"Pattie's friends were musical and they encourage Justin," explains Bruce Dale. When her friends recognized his budding talent as a percussionist, they held a local benefit to raise funds for a proper drum set. Justin wowed the crowd with some quite complicated jazz drumming—a rare feat for an eight-year-old—and the family came home with enough money to buy a bona fide drum kit. "He'd go into the furnace room and he would bang those drums like you wouldn't believe. And the worst part of it was, he was good," Dale continued.

number 51

Because he didn't have a television show, record executives didn't know what to make of Justin

His talent quickly won the skeptics over. "My first impression was, *Wow, the Macaulay Culkin of music.* He came in and he soaked up all the air in the room and he [sang] really well. But it wasn't even that. It was the face. It was the hair. He was brave. When it was all said and done, I was absolutely convinced that Usher had delivered a gift," said L.A. Reid in Justin's movie.

number

52

Being out on the road and networking is an important part of Justin's business

Before he was famous, Justin traveled all across the country visiting local radio stations and performing live for small audiences. "There's not a DJ that could say they have not met Justin Bieber," Scooter Braun says.

Bieber's rise to fame may have come quickly, but it wasn't without hard work. Ryan Good, Bieber's road manager and man-at-arms, reflects, "It went naturally, but naturally doesn't mean easy. There's work that goes into that—and you have to do the footwork."

53

Justin's film ends at a naturally high climax

The movie comes to an end with Bieber's performance in front of a sold-out crowd at Madison Square Garden in New York City. Performing at "The World's Most Famous Arena" is described as the pinnacle for a performing artist's career. Promoters were initially worried that Bieber might not get a sellout at the huge venue. He did—selling to capacity within only 22 minutes of tickets going on sale.

Never Say Never looks good on the big screen, but even better in 3D

All of the flash-whiz-bang of Justin's stage show comes through in living color like never before in *Never Say Never*. But the slick choreography, the pyrotechnics, and the larger-than-life acrobatics of his dance crew—not to mention the palpable excitement of audiences—are all the more impressive in 3-D.

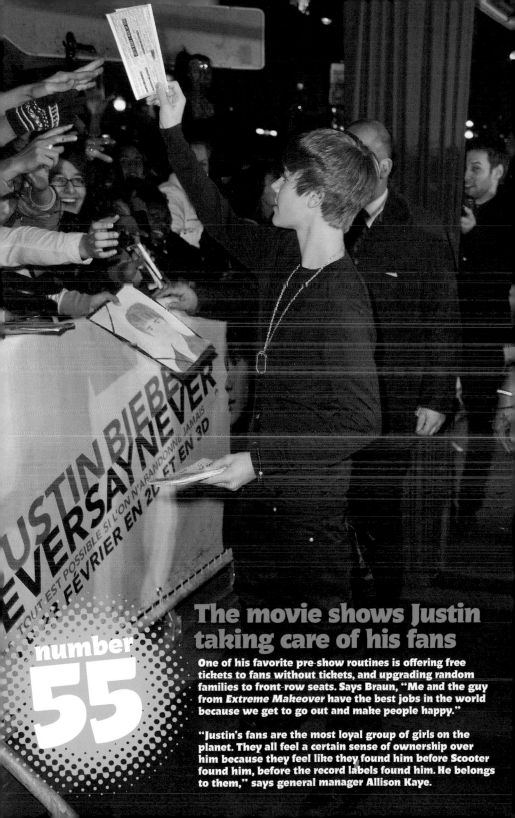

The movie shows Justin taking care of his fans

One of his favorite pre-show routines is offering free tickets to fans without tickets, and upgrading random families to front-row seats. Says Braun, "Me and the guy from *Extreme Makeover* have the best jobs in the world because we get to go out and make people happy."

"Justin's fans are the most loyal group of girls on the planet. They all feel a certain sense of ownership over him because they feel like they found him before Scooter found him, before the record labels found him. He belongs to them," says general manager Allison Kaye.

number
55

number
56

Justin even gives his fans a voice in his movie

Never Say Never not only paints a portrait of Justin as a young artist and a person, but it also puts a face to some of the countless fans who show up to concerts, buy his albums, and devote their time and attention to their favorite artist. The filmmakers give a voice to many of them, getting right to the heart of the phenomenon known as Bieber Fever and capturing the incomparable connection between the musician and his fans.

number
57

Justin is much more than just a performer on stage

He has direct communication with his army of Beliebers. When the singer goes down with what might be a tour-threatening voice loss in *Never Say Never*, get-well wishes pour in from fans across the globe. More important, Justin hits them right back, expressing his regret at having to postpone a concert date and also thanking them for their support, encouragement, and understanding.

number
58

Justin's live shows
are a spectacle

**Seeing the star himself is enough to satisfy even the
most rabid of fans. But the show itself is an impressive
undertaking—filled with incredible set pieces,
extremely complicated choreography, and plenty of
fan interaction. "I want to show that I love to perform.
There are going to be some cool tricks, some electronic
things that haven't been seen before, for sure," he told
the *Houston Chronicle* in an interview preceding the
concert. This is no Stratford Star, no YouTube living-
room performance; everything is big, overblown,**

number
59

Every show looks amazingly impressive

At one point in his live act, Justin sails high across the audience in a giant metal rig in the shape of a heart. Suspended high in the air, he belts out the song "Never Let You Go," accompanying himself on acoustic guitar. As if that's not amazing enough, the rig is actually spinning through the air! In another memorable performance moment, he cruises tantalizingly close over the heads of his audience in a giant cage as he performs the song "Up."

number 60

A magical moment occurs at every concert

Perhaps the most exciting moment—and the one that has become a signature of Justin's concerts—comes with the song "One Less Lonely Girl." For the performance, Justin chooses a single audience member from each concert and brings her on stage for a serenade. It's a romantic moment—and nearly every fan in the place waits with breathless anticipation to find out if she will be the one singled out.

number
61

The road can be quite grueling

In less than a year and a half, Justin traveled to and performed in more than 100 cities on five continents. It's a tour schedule that not only puts a strain on a person's energy, but poses serious risks to a singer's voice.

Justin found that out the hard way, when his tour hit the brakes in Syracuse in August 2010. Tired from performing in 37 cities in just over two months, and with a sore throat that seriously threatened laryngitis, the singer was forced to cancel his first show.

number

62

Justin bounces
back quickly

After cancelling a show for the first time, he was
able to appear just two days later. "I'm tough. I'm
Canadian," he tweeted. Justin credits those around
him with keeping in performance condition. Describing
Scooter Braun and Usher in his autobiography, he
writes, "They're like tag team wrestlers, only instead
of bashing me over the head with folding chairs they
make me drink lots of water."

number
63

Justin pays attention to those who came before him

He can frequently be heard pointing to his mentors who keep him focused and ready each day. One word of advice that Usher gave Justin near the beginning is something Justin can take to heart. Usher said, "Being the entertainer I am, I stand on the shoulders of giants that basically were trailblazers." It's something Justin knows all too well, and he has a massive respect for those "trailblazers" who came before him.

number

64

There's a Michael Jackson shout-out at every show

When Justin takes time to introduce his dancers and musicians one by one, they are accompanied by the sounds of Jackson's "Wanna Be Startin' Something." Justin calls it "a celebration of Michael Jackson and a good reminder for me about what matters in this business."

Jackson has undoubtedly left a huge impression on Justin as a singer and performer, but there is another legacy that is just as influential: his commitment to philanthropy. "Michael Jackson was the most giving artist of all time," Justin writes.

65

Justin is one of the most giving artists in the world

For each ticket sold on the My World 2.0 tour, one dollar was donated to Pencils of Promise. As Pencils of Promise founder Adam Braun said in an interview with the *Hollywood Reporter*, every little bit adds up. "[Scooter] and Justin were able to turn several hundred thousand fans into several hundred thousand philanthropists with each of them giving one dollar to the organization." Pencils of Promise was able to build more than 15 schools with proceeds donated from concert receipts.

66

Even when he's off the road, Justin is thinking about touring

"I have a great time performing," he told
Philadelphia radio station Q102. Touring, after all,
is the best way to connect with his millions of fans
around the world. "At the end of the day, my fans are
my everything, and they got me to this position," he
once told MTV News.

"I think I can grow as an artist, and my fans will grow
with me," he writes in his official bio. Justin shows no
signs of stopping, and neither does Bieber Fever.

number 67

Justin has the best fans in the world

As he has acknowledged every step of the way in his career, Justin's fans have paved the way for him. It was the fans, showing up in increased numbers on YouTube to comment and request more videos, who got Justin noticed by entertainment executives. It was the fans who made Justin into a multiplatinum-selling recording artist and the most powerful Twitter celebrity in the world.

number

68

Justin doesn't see himself as being powerful

The musician, who has repeatedly credited his fans with his success, sees it this way: "I don't think of myself as powerful. If anything, my fans are powerful. It's all in their hands. If they don't buy my albums, I go away," he told *Rolling Stone*.

It's not just that Justin's fans are buying his albums. They're doing so much more. Just as Justin is the trailblazing musician of the Internet age, his fans have taken their support and interaction to different levels than have ever been reached before.

number 69

It all starts with Twitter

Justin, an early adopter of the social networking site, has shown just how much can be accomplished through tweeting. He has stretched the boundaries of the medium—using it as a tour diary and window into his personality but also utilizing it as a publicity platform. His 20 million Twitter followers will be the first to hear all of his announcements—from updates on new songs and albums to tour news to charitable efforts.

Justin is extra charitable on his birthday

For his 17th birthday, Justin announced his affiliation with the nonprofit organization Charity:Water, and wrote on the charity's website, "This year, I really want my birthday to be all about helping others. Instead of asking for gifts, I'm asking friends, family, and fans to consider donating $17 for my 17th birthday to help make a change. One hundred percent of all donations go directly to building clean water projects in developing countries." The program was such a success he repeated it for his 18th birthday.

Fans rally behind Justin like no other singer

In September 2011 a prankster made false copyright claims to YouTube, alleging that the official Justin Bieber channel (along with official channels for fellow artists Lady Gaga and Rihanna, among others) was broadcasting unauthorized content. YouTube's official policy is to pull any content in dispute, and the channel disappeared. Almost immediately, a posse of Bieber fans were on the case, and helped to bring the false claim to YouTube's attention and resolve the issue quickly.

The army of Beliebers is a force all its own

Fans from all over the world have paid tribute to Justin, creating Web sites devoted to the musician and his music; posting YouTube tribute videos, fan fiction, and poetry; and creating online communities where fans can congregate and communicate with one another.

They've also shown their numbers physically, gathering wherever the star goes. Beliebers in Newcastle, England, celebrating the star's arrival before his upcoming concert, began an impromptu parade down the city's streets, singing Bieber's music and promenading through the city with signs and banners heralding his arrival.

Sometimes, the army of fans can be crushing

The crowd of fans awaiting a performance in Australia swelled so large outside the gates that it turned into a stampede. Police were forced to postpone the performance. "I am just as disappointed as everyone else with the news from this morning. I want to sing for my fans," Bieber tweeted. "I woke up this morning to the police canceling the show for safety reasons.... I love my fans.... I love it here in Australia...and I want to sing." A similar near-riot broke out months earlier at Roosevelt Field Mall in Long Island, New York.

The singer said, "I think it's my fans being really supportive.... At the end of the day, my fans are my everything, and they got me to this position."

number 74

Justin's on-stage look is carefully crafted

Unlike the pop idols of his youth—like Boyz II Men, with their carefully choreographed and well-scrubbed styles—there's something of an edge to the clothes Justin wears on stage. It all starts with Ryan Good, Justin's so-called "swagger coach" and stylist.

For most of his tours, his on-stage ensemble has a heavy element of street style and highlights the singer's signature color: purple.

number
75

Hip-hop is a major influence on Justin's style

Justin wears a white denim jacket embellished with straps and metal hardware. The look is heavily influenced by hip-hop elements. Paired with white jeans speckled with purple, the look is crisp but definitely not clean-cut. A studded belt picks up the stud accents on his jacket and ties together the look. Add a splash of purple from the hoodie layered underneath, plus the purple Supra Skytop sneakers and a purple baseball cap (his dancers wear the same purple cap, too) and the look is complete. It's a look that's unmistakably Bieber.

number
76

Justin's shoes are in a museum

Justin has become known for his preference for Supra sneakers, and a well-worn pair that he broke in on stage was enshrined in Toronto's Bata Shoe Museum. The museum, which features shoes worn by such musical notables as John Lennon and Madonna, hosts a collection of footwear from throughout the ages—everything from Napoleon Bonaparte's socks to Queen Victoria's slippers. Talk about putting your best foot forward!

number

77

Hats are an important part of Justin's style

Whether on stage or just hanging out, he's often sporting a hat. Most often, it's a baseball cap. Often, it's in support of the New York Yankees baseball team. Besides the Yankees' traditional blue, the singer has donned turquoise, black, and purple versions of the cap. But don't assume he's a die-hard fanatic of the Bronx Bombers; he's also worn ballcaps for his now-hometown Atlanta Braves, as well as the Detroit Tigers.

number
78

Glasses are a fairly recent addition to Justin's accessories

The singer has showcased a wide array of spectacles on the red carpet and on the street. He's rocked huge, chunky-framed eyeglasses and other spectacles in black and white. He has recently been seen sporting wire-rimmed specs, as featured at the 2011 VMAs. The singer reportedly has perfect vision; the glasses are purely a style choice. He's also often seen in sunglasses, a true staple accessory for any celebrity.

79

Dating Selena has changed Justin's style

She is an established fashionista and bona fide sophisticate. The two first glammed it up as a couple when they stepped out for the first time together—to no dressier an occasion than the Oscar post-parties. In an interview before the 2011 MTV Video Music Awards, Selena interviewed Justin about his red-carpet fashion. The singer walked the white carpet wearing a dressed-up but very rock 'n' roll look, including a Yves St. Laurent tuxedo jacket, brooch, and cheetah-print sneakers paired with red pants. Perhaps Selena's taste for couture is rubbing off on him.

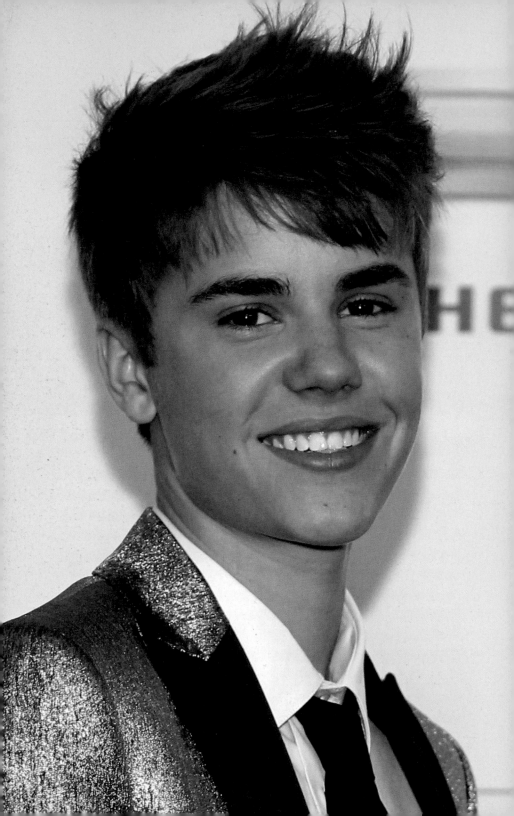

number

80

Justin's hair is some of the most famous in the world

Justin's famous 'do has been the subject of countless ruminations. It was even adapted into a wig—a hot-selling costume accessory. Bieber's hairstylist, Vanessa Price, had a big hand in shaping the performer's forward-swept style. And when he decided to change it, Price was there, scissors in hand.

"thinking about getting a haircut....hmmmmmm," the singer tweeted to his fans on February 21, 2011. The singer, known for his practical joking, had fans on the ropes. Was he serious? It turns out he was!

number
81

The Bieber brand is everywhere

To put it simply, Bieber is a household name in every sense of the term. Forget the fashion. Bieber's official website offers gadgets and gizmos for every Belieber in your life. Got a friend who's positively attached to her phone? You've got your choice of Bieber-themed iPhone skins. What about that person on your list who loves to travel? Why not pick up the Justin Bieber Travel Kit—or better yet, the singing toothbrush that croons "Somebody to Love" and "Love Me" as you brush your pearly whites.

Though he doesn't wear it, Justin has a nail polish line

Working with cosmetic giant OPI, each nail polish shade bears a name inspired by one of Justin's songs. From "One Less Lonely Glitter" to "Prized Possession Purple" and "Step 2 the Beat of My Heart." The shades were an instant hit for Wal-Mart, the exclusive retailer, selling more than 1 million bottles in their first month and selling out nationwide. The line has since expanded from its initial six shades to 14 different colors, and is now available in stores across the nation.

number

83

Other celebrities love teaming with Biebs

Justin teamed with legendary rapper Dr. Dre to release his own brand of Beats, the Dre-developed headphones that have become increasingly popular in the digital music age. Justin's Beats are—surprise!— purple and chrome. Touted with the tagline "sound is the emotion between us," the headphones come in on-ear and in-ear varieties.

And if that collaboration isn't surprising enough, he's also recently signed with the Middleton family (yes, as in Princess Kate!), who own an online party-planning business called Party Pieces. The website purchased rights to sell the "Justin Bieber Ultimate Party Kit," a veritable Bieber party in a box.

number
84

Justin is one of the hottest spokesmen on the market

For the ad blitz of Super Bowl XLV—with commercials going for a pretty penny at $3 million for a 30-second spot—Best Buy ran an ad with Justin and famous rocker Ozzy Osbourne. The commercial, a play on the technology gap between generations, ended up being one of the most memorable—and hilarious—of the day.

One might think that with all these products and advertisements out on the market, Justin has reached his media-saturation point, but his Q score—the standard numeric index of a celebrity's popularity, as used by advertisers—remains on solid footing.

number
85

Video games are a favorite distraction for Justin

He mainly plays Xbox and is a fan of the video game system's offerings, most recently NBA 2K, Call of Duty: Modern Warfare 2, Marvel vs. DC, and Madden 2012. His head of security Kenny Hamilton is "a frequent victim of [his] Xbox 360 powers of annihilation," as Justin wrote in his memoir. Justin is able to keep up with his favorite game franchises every year during downtime on his tours.

number

86

Justin is humble and giving

With a vast team of managers, producers, crew, and other entourage members surrounding them, it's tempting for artists to believe that the world revolves around them. Justin Bieber is not one of those artists. He has shown time and again that he is committed to giving back. And he gives and gives—not only through financial contributions but with his time. For a kid whose own grueling touring schedule and other commitments already wear him thin, his insistence on making charity a top priority is commendable.

number 87

Justin is well-respected in the world of philanthropy

His tireless philanthropic efforts earned him a 2010 Do Something Award and a 2010 Power of Youth Philanthropy Award from *Variety*— impressive accolades for the then-16-year-old. The awards recognized not only the singer's personal contributions, but also the influence he had on others to get involved. Indeed, Justin's charitable spirit has caused a ripple effect throughout his fan base, galvanizing a whole generation of Beliebers to think globally about giving.

number
88

Some tracks Justin sings on are for charity

In January 2010 a devastating earthquake hit the island of Haiti, causing widespread destruction and claiming more than 300,000 lives. Artists across the United States answered the call, recording a new version of "We Are the World" to help raise funds to aid rebuilding efforts. The original song, written by Lionel Richie and Michael Jackson and conceived as a charitable effort to send aid to a poverty-stricken Africa, became the top-selling single of all-time. In the 25th anniversary version, Justin was given the honor of the song's opening solo. Benefiting the Red Cross, the new single brought much-needed funds to tragedy-stricken Haitians.

169

number

89

Justin contributes whole songs to charity

When Mother Nature struck again—this time, in the form of an earthquake and tsunami that decimated wide swaths of Japan—Justin again felt the call. Teaming with many artists, Bieber lent a version of his song "Pray" to the album *Songs for Japan*. The proceeds went straight to the Japanese Red Cross and its rebuilding efforts.

Justin wrote, "I am in the position to give back thanks to my fans and God. I wrote the track 'Pray' thinking I wanted to help others and I feel like I have a responsibility to do so. What is the point of doing all this if you can't make a difference in others' lives?"

number
90

Kids are the main focus of Justin's charity efforts

In addition to Pencils of Promise, he is aligned with the Make-A-Wish Foundation, which grants "wishes" to hospitalized children, many of whom suffer from terminal diseases. He often visits with its children at his concerts and in hospitals. "It's just crazy that I'm a wish," he told CNN.

He has also worked with It Gets Better, a nonprofit organization raising awareness and providing counsel for victims of bullying, and has helped join the movement to warn against the often fatal consequences of texting and driving.

Date _____ December 21, 20

Children's Wish

PROJECT MEDISHARE

500,000 %

number
91

Charity comes naturally to Justin

There are myriad causes and organizations to which Justin has contributed his attention—too many to name here. One thing is for certain: in a short time, he has established a considerable legacy for himself.

"For me it goes past the money," he told CNN. "I have such a big platform. It would be silly if I didn't do something good with it."

92

Justin lends a part of himself—literally—to some charity efforts

A pair of rhinestone embellished Supras sold on eBay to benefit the Ovarian Cancer Research Fund. He also took a lock of hair from his famous hair cut and sold it on the auction site. Proceeds from that famed lock of hair raised more than $40,000 for a variety of charitable organizations.

Recently, he has partnered with Give Back Brands to develop his fragrance, Someday. One hundred percent of net proceeds from the perfume sale have gone straight to multiple charities.

number
93

Being so good at so many things is a rare feat for a teenager

Being successful in multiple pursuits is incredibly difficult in life. It takes a massive amount of commitment to get there. Jada Pinkett Smith should know. Her husband leveraged early fame as a rapper and a hugely successful adult recording artist and Oscar-nominated actor. "[Bieber is like] a little Will Smith. He's so passionate about what he does and he does it for his fans," Jada Pinkett Smith said to Chelsea Handler in an interview.

number
94

Justin has the intangible 'it' factor

"He was born a star," Usher told *Time* magazine. "He knew what he wanted to accomplish; all he had to do was get everyone else to believe it.... Stay tuned, because his story will get even better."

"I think he's the kid who [will] go beyond the teenage puppy-love thing; he's the kid that they grow with. He's special," says L.A. Reid in *Justin Bieber: Never Say Never*.

Usher agrees. "As he grows, as he goes through life's experiences, as he loves, as he finds relationships. All of this will become a part of the story, and for me it's beautiful to watch."

number
95

FEBRUARY

Being raised on the road is tough, but it's easier with such a good 'family'

Justin's team, or "family," as he calls his inner circle, have a professional ambition to see their artist succeed, but they also feel a strong personal commitment to the singer's upbringing. "Ninety percent of my job is making sure he becomes a good man. That's a family," says manager Scooter Braun in *Justin Bieber: Never Say Never.*

Having his road family and his mom with him at every step along the way has been crucial in keeping the musician grounded. The component of faith—Justin leads a prayer vigil before each show—is another strong foundation.

96

Justin will never give up

Justin has no plans to hold back. "I know that to be the best I can be will take a lot of work. I know I have to give up a lot of myself, or a lot of a private life. But the saying 'Practice makes perfect,' really does make sense. The more you practice, the better you get," Justin told *Vanity Fair*.

number

97

The future looks promising

When asked what he sees for himself in the future, Justin said, "I see myself just growing. I didn't know that any of this was really possible. I grew up in a really small town with not a lot of money, and I liked singing, but it was just something that was a hobby. And as I get into it more, I want to grow as an artist, as an entertainer, and basically perfect my craft. I want to be the best that I can be."

number

98

Justin and Selena are still going strong

Ever since they first admitted that they were dating in March of 2011, Justin and Selena Gomez have been one of entertainment's hottest couples. She is almost two years older than Justin and the two have been spotted getting very romantic whenever they have a chance to spend time together. Dating someone else with a busy schedule and a public image helps make their relationship go smoother, and judging by how close they looked on the video set for "Boyfriend," things are going smoother than ever.

number
99

Justin is an awesome big brother

Justin's little sister Jasmine absolutely adores her big brother and the feeling is mutual! She's just a toddler but is very smart and outgoing, making her first TV appearance in a behind-the-scenes clip when she ran on stage during one of her brother's interviews for *Never Say Never*. She spent some time chasing her brother around the stage as Justin played along, making the most of his limited time with his loved ones. Last Christmas she even came on stage and helped Justin sing "Baby."

Justin is one heck of an athlete

He first showed off his athletic skills in public when he dropped into a celebrity game during the NBA's All-Star weekend. Playing against friends like Romeo Miller (a former college player) and Hall of Famer Scottie Pippen, Biebs stole the show with his flashy dribbling and outside shooting and was named MVP. As a Canadian, his first love is hockey and he has been spotted skating with members of his hometown Toronto Maple Leafs. During a European tour he showed off his skills in another one of his favorites, training with famous soccer teams Chelsea and Barcelona.